Charles Lindbergh

Charles Lindbergh

Pilot

LUCIA RAATMA

Ferguson Publishing Company
Chicago, Illinois

Photographs ©:AP/Wideworld: 8, 28, 30, 32, 37, 39, 43, 50, 52, 53, 55, 58, 61, 63, 64, 70, 71, 73, 76, 79, 81, 82, 88, 94, 95; Archive Photos: 12, 15, 56, 85; Corbis: 10, 23, 69; Liaison Agency: cover, 97, 98.

An Editorial Directions Book

ISBN 0-89434-340-8
Copyright © 2000 by Ferguson Publishing Company
Published and distributed by
Ferguson Publishing Company
200 West Jackson Boulevard, Suite 700
Chicago, Illinois 60606
www.fergpubco.com

Printed in the United States of America

X-8

CONTENTS

A LANDING
IN PARIS

WHEN CHARLES LINDBERGH landed his plane at Paris's Le Bourget Airport in May 1927, he had done something special. He had become the first person to make a solo nonstop flight across the Atlantic Ocean. Flying planes was still a new idea, and flying across the ocean was very dangerous.

Lindbergh had planned well for the trip. He had worked hard at flying school, and he learned all he could about his plane, the *Spirit of St. Louis*. His diligence and determination had paid off.

Crowds of people had been waiting for Lindbergh to land in Paris. They rushed onto the runway to meet him.

Although many others had tried to fly such a long distance without stopping, no one had succeeded. Some got lost, and others were forced to turn back. But Lindbergh was successful. So when he landed in Paris, he was instantly famous. Reporters flocked around him, and crowds of people came to the airport in hopes of meeting him. He was seen as a hero.

This important flight from New York to Paris is the event for which Charles Lindbergh is best known. But his career as a pilot had many parts. As a young man, he barnstormed in the Midwest, performing daring tricks in the air. He also carried airmail and served in the Air Service Reserve Corps. Later in his life, he helped make better planes and promoted the field of aviation. For Charles Lindbergh, flying was more important than fame.

Charles A. Lindbergh at the age of fourteen months. As he grew up, so did the world of aviation.

EYES ON THE SKY

CHARLES AUGUSTUS LINDBERGH grew up in two worlds. Part of the year, he lived on his family's farm outside Little Falls, Minnesota. For the rest of the year, he lived in Washington, D.C., because his father, Charles August (C.A.) was a United States congressman. Because he grew up in these two places, Charles had both a strong love of the outdoors and a good understanding of politics.

Born on February 4, 1902, in Detroit, Michigan, Charles arrived just as aviation was coming into being. Only one year later, in

Young Charles with his father, C.A. The elder Lindbergh served as a U.S. congressman for much of his son's childhood.

1903, brothers Wilbur and Orville Wright would make the first plane flight. As Charles grew up, so did the field of aviation. He was to play a very important role in that industry.

Early Interests

As a young boy, Charles was interested in anything mechanical. He often worked on farm equipment and even took his bicycle apart and put it back together again. He enjoyed seeing how things worked.

Once, when he was eight years old, a loud noise distracted him while he was getting ready to meet some of his friends. It was a plane flying over his house! Charles was so excited that he climbed out on the roof and waved to the pilot. He kept his eyes on the sky and watched as the plane flew over. Right then, he said to himself, "Someday I'm going to fly."

At Grandfather's

In addition to spending time on the farm and in Washington, Charles enjoyed visiting his grandfather in Detroit. He would often go there with his mother, Evangeline, in the summer. Charles's grandfather was a dentist and inventor, even though he never finished high school. He taught himself about science and was always eager to learn new things.

In his grandfather's laboratory, Charles watched the older man work. He helped out when he could and asked lots of questions. He admired the things his grandfather could do with his hands. Charles wanted to be good with his hands, too.

The Model T

When Charles was eleven, his father, C.A., bought a Model T Ford. As soon as his feet could reach the pedals, young Charles drove the car around the Minnesota countryside. He drove his mother on picnics and picked up his father from the train station. Before long, he learned all he could about the automobile. He could change flat tires, make small repairs, and adjust the carburetor.

In the meantime, C.A. worried about whether the United States should become involved in World War I (1914–1918). C.A. believed that big companies were pushing the country to enter the war just so they could make money. Charles drove his father from town to town as the congressman tried to explain his views to the voters.

The Lindbergh home in Little Falls, Minnesota. The house is now part of the Charles A. Lindbergh State Park.

A few years later, after C.A. lost the election, he was no longer a member of Congress. C.A. decided to stay in Washington, although the rest of the family no longer had to live there. Evangeline was pleased, and she immediately planned a trip to

California. She wanted to take the train, but four-teen-year-old Charles convinced her to let him drive. So Charles and Evangeline set out for California. It was a 1,500-mile (2,414-kilometer) trip, and Charles drove the entire way.

In and Out of School

Through the years, Charles never spent much time in any one school. Living in two different places meant he seldom stayed in one school for long. So much moving around, combined with Charles's lack of interest in academics, made him a rather poor student. But books really didn't interest Charles. He wanted to experience the world firsthand, not read about it. He didn't have the patience to study and keep up with his school requirements.

When Charles was sixteen, it looked as though he would not graduate from high school. But that year, the government created a new program. Any high-school senior who wanted to drop out of school and work on a farm could do so and still graduate. This program was offered because many farms were short of workers while men were off fighting in World War I. Charles jumped at the chance to work outside all day rather than finish school. His mother gave him permission, and he got his diploma.

For two years, Charles ran the family farm. He bought and repaired machinery. He milked cows, tended sheep, plowed the fields, and kept the barn neat and clean. He learned to be responsible and handle many tasks on his own. This independence would serve him well in later years.

Moving On

Charles had vowed that someday he would fly. But he still didn't know what he wanted to do with his life. His mother urged him to go to college. She felt it was very important, and Charles decided to try it. In the fall of 1920, he entered the University of Wisconsin. He majored in engineering because he loved mechanical things. But he soon realized that college wasn't the answer for him.

BECOMING A PILOT

J UST AS IN high school, Lindbergh didn't find his college courses interesting. He was bored and, instead of studying, he rode his new motorcycle all over the countryside. Before long, the University of Wisconsin put Charles Lindbergh on academic probation.

Lindbergh thought that many of his classmates were immature. He had little in common with them because they drank and smoked. His only college-related interest was the Reserve Officers Training Corps (ROTC). He was a member of the ROTC pistol and rifle team. His team placed first in a national competition.

No Fear

One of the best-known stories from Lindbergh's college years is about an incident that actually took place off campus. Charles and two of his friends were riding their motorcycles when they came to the top of a steep hill. His friends said that a rider would definitely need brakes to go down that hill. Lindbergh said he could do it without using his brakes. His friends scoffed, but he was determined to prove them wrong.

The first time Lindbergh went down the hill without using his brakes, he crashed into a fence when he tried to make a turn. He stood up and looked at the hill. He considered the mechanics of the motorcycle—determined never to back down from a challenge—and suddenly knew what he had done wrong. Then he checked his bike for damage. It seemed fine to him, so he tried again. On the second attempt, he didn't slow down as he had done before. Instead, he gunned the engine as he came to the bottom of the hill. He made the turn safely without using his brakes.

Ready to Fly

By the middle of his sophomore year, Lindbergh was sure the university was about to dismiss him and decided to leave before that happened. A friend told him about an airplane company that offered flying lessons. Lindbergh knew he wanted to go.

His parents were opposed to his plan. They said flying was dangerous and worried that he would get hurt. But Lindbergh was stubborn. In March 1922, he left the University of Wisconsin, got on his motorcycle, and rode to Ray Page's Flying School in Lincoln, Nebraska.

Into the Air

Lindbergh quickly learned all he could about the school's airplanes. He asked the mechanics questions and helped out with repairs as much as possible. Lindbergh knew that understanding how planes worked would help him fly them. They nicknamed him "Slim" at the flying school.

On April 9, 1922, Slim finally made it into the air and was thrilled by the experience. In his book *The Spirit of St. Louis*, he remembers how he felt in the air: "I lose all conscious connection with the past. I live only in the moment in this strange, unmortal [*sic*] space, crowded with beauty, pierced with danger."

Unfortunately, Lindbergh's instructor, Ira Biffle, had lost his enthusiasm for flying after a good friend had died in a crash. He was beginning to fear airplanes and began to make up excuses to cancel lessons. Lindbergh was frustrated by Biffle's worries. And Biffle was the only instructor at the flying school. In addition, Ray Page had decided to sell his only training plane. Lindbergh knew it was time to move on.

Daredevil

Ray Page sold his airplane to Erold Bahl, a pilot who wanted flying to be taken more seriously. Lindbergh saw his chance and asked Bahl for a job. Before long, Lindbergh was Bahl's assistant and had an active role in the new practice of barnstorming.

Barnstormers did stunts in small planes, usually over open fields and farms. During the 1920s, many people knew nothing about flying or were afraid of airplanes. Barnstorming attracted large crowds and showed flying to be a thrilling activity. The performances introduced many people to aviation and proved how sturdy the planes were.

A stuntman walking on the wing of a Curtiss JN-4D Jenny. Lindbergh worked as a wing walker and barnstormer after leaving college.

One stunt Lindbergh performed was wing walking. While the plane was in the air, Lindbergh would walk out on one of its wings and wave to the crowds on the ground below. Another trick was parachute jumping. On his first try, Lindbergh even completed a double jump. For a double jump, he had two parachutes attached to him. As he fell, the first parachute would open and then was cut away. He would then free-fall until the second parachute opened—just before he reached the ground. The crowd loved these exciting stunts.

Lindbergh learned all about parachuting. He learned how to land, even in bad conditions, and he learned how to avoid injury. This knowledge would be very important for Lindbergh in the years to come.

Beyond Barnstorming

During the summer of 1922, Lindbergh worked as a barnstormer throughout the Midwest. Crowds knew his name and looked forward to performances by "Daredevil Lindbergh." Lindbergh was enjoying himself, but he knew he wanted to do more. Most of all, he wanted to fly the plane, not just do stunts.

The following year, Lindbergh bought his first plane. It was a "Jenny," the nickname for a World War I Curtiss JN-4D. Soon he flew his first solo flight. He then learned how to do spins, rolls, and dives and became a stunt flier. Entertaining crowds was fun for Lindbergh, and he had learned a lot during his barnstorming days. But he still wanted to be a serious pilot.

A Student Again

In March 1924, Lindbergh entered the Army Air Service training school in San Antonio, Texas. Lindbergh spent many hours flying during his year there. He also spent many hours in the classroom, too. He studied late at night and on weekends. Learning about flight was important to him, so he worked as hard as he could.

He later remembered, "I'd really gotten down to business, worked on my studies as I had never worked before. I hadn't been much impressed by university diplomas. . . . But an Air Service pilot's wings were like a silver passport to the realm of flight." He was 1 of 104 students when he began his studies, and 1 of only 18 who graduated. He was at the top of his class.

Finally, Lindbergh had received the training he had always wanted. He was a pilot, a goal for which he had long worked. His next task was deciding how to use his skills in a worthwhile career.

MAKING HISTORY 4

THE UNITED STATES began sending letters by airmail in 1918. Carrying airmail was such a dangerous job that thirty-one of the first forty airmail pilots were killed in plane crashes. When airmail service began, the U.S. Post Office was in charge. But in 1925, the responsibility was given to private companies.

Delivering the Mail

William and Frank Robertson, the owners of Robertson Aircraft Corporation, had a contract to deliver airmail between St. Louis and

Chicago. In early 1925, Lindbergh happened to be in St. Louis, and the Robertsons heard about him. The brothers met Lindbergh at an international air race. Having been fliers in World War I, they appreciated good pilots. They were very impressed by Lindbergh's skill and his serious attitude.

Lindbergh in a Robertson plane. The owners of Robertson Aircraft Corporation trusted him with delivering the mail.

By then, Lindbergh was considered to be one of the country's finest pilots. He was known for being mentally focused and for preparing well for his flights. He was also a strong young man in good physical shape. The Robertsons took all of his attributes into account and offered him a job. They asked Lindbergh to be chief pilot of their airmail route, and Lindbergh was eager for the challenge.

Facing Danger

As an airmail pilot in these early days, Lindbergh faced many problems. First, the planes used for delivering mail were badly designed. Some people called them "flaming coffins" because they caught fire easily during emergency landings. Second, the weather often made flying dangerous. Pilots flew through snow, sleet, rain, and fog. Getting weather reports was often impossible, so pilots had to decide on their own whether it was safe to fly. Third, at that time, pilots had no radio communication with anyone on the ground. They had no way to get help if they were lost or in trouble.

In spite of these dangers, Lindbergh was a very successful airmail pilot. He hired two other pilots and supervised them and their delivery routes. They

Being an airmail pilot was a dangerous job. Lindbergh's plane crashed on a number of occasions.

made five round-trip flights a week. Over the years, their record for being on time was impressive, but still the pilots had many problems. They often had to make emergency landings. Sometimes they had to parachute out of the planes, carrying the bags of mail with them. The tricks Lindbergh had picked up as a barnstormer and as a flight student proved very important.

Lindbergh developed many safety procedures on his own. When parachuting, he kept his legs crossed. This way he would not accidentally straddle wires or tree branches as he fell toward the ground. When he made emergency landings, he flew low for as long as possible. That used up more fuel and helped avoid an explosion upon landing.

His job as chief pilot gave him many opportunities to think about difficult situations. It taught him to think quickly and to be as prepared as possible for any problem. These were important skills for Lindbergh to develop as he approached his most famous flight.

The Orteig Prize

Raymond Orteig was a Frenchman who owned the Brevoort and Lafayette Hotels in New York City. In 1919, when aviation was still very young, he offered a prize of $25,000 to the first person to fly nonstop from New York to Paris—or from Paris to New York. The offer was good for five years. After the five years passed and the prize had not been won, Orteig extended his offer for another five years.

By the fall of 1926, a number of pilots were considering the flight. Among them was René Fonck, a

René Fonck was one of the pilots who had set their sights on the Orteig Prize. He was a French flier who had served in World War I.

French pilot who had served in World War I. Another hopeful was Richard Byrd, the first man to fly over the North Pole. As Lindbergh heard about the other pilots' plans, he reminded himself of all he had already accomplished. He asked himself: "Why shouldn't I fly from New York to Paris? I'm almost twenty-five. I have more than four years of aviation behind me, and close to 2,000 hours in the air. I've barnstormed over half the forty-eight states [Alaska and Hawaii were not yet states]. I've flown my mail through the worst of nights." Why wouldn't a flight across the ocean prove as possible as all these things have been? And then Lindbergh made up his mind. He would plan a flight to Paris.

Plans into Action

First, Lindbergh had to get people to sponsor him for the trip. He needed money for a plane and for other supplies. Lindbergh's good reputation made it easy to find support. At this point, he was living in St. Louis, Missouri. He had started giving flying lessons to Harry Knight, the president of the St. Louis Flying Club. Lindbergh told Knight about his dream of flying to Paris, and Knight thought Lindbergh could succeed.

Knight introduced the young pilot to Harold Bixby, the head of the St. Louis Chamber of Commerce. Lindbergh convinced Bixby that if his flight were successful, it would strengthen St. Louis's image as a flight center. So, Bixby and a group of other men decided to back Lindbergh. They agreed to a budget of $15,000 and named Lindbergh's plane the *Spirit of St. Louis*.

The Right Plane

Now Lindbergh had to find a plane. Many people thought that the new multiengine planes were safer than single-engine ones. The idea was that if one engine failed, the others would keep the plane in the air. Lindbergh disagreed, however. He felt that a single-engine plane was a better option for a flight over the ocean. It would be lighter than a multiengine plane. Less weight meant that less fuel would be used, so he could fly for a longer time. Also, many believed that pilots needed to fly with a navigator. Again, Lindbergh disagreed. Flying alone meant less weight in the plane. Lindbergh stood his ground and convinced his backers that his should be a one-engine, one-pilot flight.

Lindbergh heard of a single-engine plane for sale

from the Columbia Aircraft Corporation in New York. Unfortunately, the company wanted to charge $15,000—Lindbergh's entire budget. And that price didn't even include an engine! He contacted his backers, and they approved the amount. But when Lindbergh arrived in New York to buy the plane, he met with disappointment. He learned that the company president, Charles Levine, wanted to choose the pilot and crew for the flight. Lindbergh said that he would fly the plane or the deal was off. So he went back to St. Louis without a plane.

When 1927 rolled around, Lindbergh was still searching for the right plane. Finally, his hopes were answered. Ryan Airlines Corporation in San Diego, California, heard about Lindbergh's problem and offered to build him a plane. Their price tag was only $6,000 (also without an engine) but they needed three months to do the job. Lindbergh was encouraged though and set off for San Diego.

Once he arrived at Ryan headquarters, Lindbergh was again a little worried. Their building was old and in bad repair. It had once been a fish cannery and it still smelled of fish. But after meeting with company president Frank Mahoney and chief engineer and designer Donald Hall, Lindbergh knew he was in good hands. These two men were very confident, and they were dedicated to building the right plane for Lindbergh. They even agreed, at Lindbergh's insistence, to finish in two months instead of three. Mahoney and Hall seemed to know that they were becoming a part of something very special.

Spirit of St. Louis

Lindbergh worked with Mahoney and Hall for the next several weeks. Their goal was to make the *Spirit of St. Louis* the perfect plane to fly to Paris. Hall seldom left the Ryan building. He and his staff worked many hours of overtime. They did all they could to ensure the success of the project.

Lindbergh was consulted about the design details. He approved the addition of more fuel tanks to the plane so that he could safely complete the long flight. To accommodate this extra weight, the plane's wingspan was increased. It was estimated that his range would be at least 4,000 miles (6,436 km). Lindbergh and his team also decided to place the fuel tank in front of the pilot's seat instead of in back. This way, Lindbergh would not get caught between the engine and the fuel tank during an

Charles Lindbergh with Frank Mahoney (left). Mahoney was the president of Ryan Airlines Corporation, which built the Spirit of St. Louis.

emergency landing. However, the tank's position would block part of his forward vision. Lindbergh was not concerned by this. He convinced the designers that he could look out the side windows as needed.

Keeping the plane light remained Lindbergh's biggest concern. He decided to leave many items behind, considering them unnecessary or too heavy. These items included a parachute, a radio, gas gauges, and navigation lights. He even trimmed down his maps, so that they included only the reference points he needed. Finally, he decided that a regular leather pilot's chair was too heavy. Instead, he had a light wicker chair placed in the cockpit.

No doubt, these design decisions were risky. To decrease the plane's weight, Lindbergh had opted to do without many safety items. Few pilots would have taken such a risk. But Lindbergh trusted in his own knowledge and listened to his instincts.

On April 28, 1927, the *Spirit of St. Louis* was completed. When empty, it weighed 2,150 pounds (976 kg). It was 9 feet, 8 inches (2.9 m) in height and 27 feet, 8 inches (8.4 m) long. It had a wingspan of 46 feet (14 m) and an engine that was expected to per-

Lindbergh with his plane, the Spirit of St. Louis, *completed on April 28, 1927.*

form for more than 9,000 hours. At last, Charles Lindbergh had his plane.

Competition

During the plane's construction, Lindbergh had worried that another pilot would beat him across the

Atlantic. As the months passed, however, no one succeeded. René Fonck's plane crashed during takeoff,
killing two crew members. Fonck and his navigator
survived. When Richard Byrd crashed during a test
flight, his backers asked for more tests, so Byrd's trip
was delayed.

Another pilot, Clarence Chamberlin, became
involved in a legal dispute. His plane was locked up,
and he was not allowed to take off. Meanwhile, pilot
Noel Davis crashed after just getting off the ground.
Davis and his copilot, Stanton Wooster, were killed.
Then, just days before Lindbergh planned to fly from
San Diego to New York, the radio reported the start of
another transatlantic flight.

Frenchmen Charles Nungesser and François Coli
had taken off from Paris and were headed toward
New York. Reports said that they had been sighted
over the Atlantic. Lindbergh feared he was too late.
But the reports that the Frenchmen were close to
the U.S. coast were wrong. Sadly, Nungesser and
Coli were never seen again.

Final Preparations

On May 10, 1927, Lindbergh flew from San Diego to
St. Louis. The trip took fourteen hours and broke

records for the longest and fastest nonstop flight. Then, after a day's rest, he flew to Curtiss Field on Long Island, New York.

Once he landed in New York, reporters began to overwhelm Lindbergh. Suddenly, he was no longer an unknown pilot. Instead, he was a shy, attractive young man who was being hounded by the press. Everywhere he went, bright camera lights and dozens of questions followed him. The press called him "Lucky Lindy" or "The Lone Eagle." He did not like the nicknames and found the attention unpleasant. He was hardly ever asked about aviation or his skills. Instead, the reporters questioned him about which girls he liked and other personal matters. He later wrote, "Contacts with the press became increasingly distasteful to me. I felt that interviews and photographs tended to confuse and cheapen life. . . ."

But Lindbergh knew he had serious matters to handle. He studied maps and performed test flights. He studied the weather and waited for the right conditions. While the young pilot was busy with his preparations, however, Richard Byrd and Clarence Chamberlin were also readying themselves for flight.

No More Waiting

For several days, the weather kept Lindbergh and the others on the ground. Nova Scotia reported dense fog, and it had been raining in New York. Finally, Lindbergh got word that a high-pressure system was moving through the region. This system would cause the weather to clear. The time was right.

Lindbergh had originally planned to take off from Curtiss Field, but then he decided that the runway at Curtiss Field was too short. He wanted to use Roosevelt Field, instead, which was very close by. But Roosevelt Field's runway was longer only because Richard Byrd had made it so. And Byrd had exclusive rights to use Roosevelt Field. Nevertheless, upon hearing of Lindbergh's wish to use Roosevelt, Byrd offered him the runway. His show of good sportsmanship had historic importance.

The night before his flight, Lindbergh tried to sleep. But noise in his hotel kept him awake, and he got no sleep at all.

He arrived at Roosevelt Field on the morning of May 20, 1927. It was still rainy and misty. The runway was muddy. The wind had changed direction, so the tailwind he wanted was not there. He would

Wishing him well on the historic flight. Lindbergh with fellow pilots Richard Byrd (center) and Clarence Chamberlain (right).

have to fly into the wind. But in spite of the imperfect conditions, he was ready to go.

Lindbergh checked his plane carefully. He checked the wings, the propeller, and the brakes. He noted that the tanks were full of gasoline. The tires of the plane bulged from the weight of the fuel. For a moment, he worried a little about the power lines he would have to fly over when he took off. Then he worried about the muddy runway. But still he decided the time was right.

The Historic Takeoff

Satisfied with the condition of his plane, Lindbergh put his flying suit on over his clothes. As a crowd of people watched, he put on his helmet and goggles. Finally, he climbed into the cockpit, settled into the wicker chair, and looked at the controls. Then he signaled the Roosevelt Field crewmen to start turning the propeller.

The plane's engine roared to life. Lindbergh lowered his goggles and pulled his safety belt on tight. The plane slowly moved forward. A car carrying three men with fire extinguishers followed Lindbergh down the runway. Fortunately, they were not needed. Lindbergh pulled back on the throttle, and the *Spirit of St. Louis* rose, clearing the power lines by 20 feet (6.2 m).

It was 7:52 A.M., and Lindbergh was headed for Paris.

A Long Flight

Once Lindbergh was in the air, he faced many more challenges. He flew over the New England states and Canada. Then he flew over Nova Scotia and Newfoundland. After hours and hours had passed, he was above the vast, dark Atlantic Ocean.

He looked at the moon and stars against the black sky. Sitting in that plane at that moment, he must have felt very much alone. Many people had helped him prepare for the flight, but now only his own endurance and determination would get him to Paris safely.

Suddenly Lindbergh found himself within a storm cloud. The cloud surrounded the *Spirit of St. Louis,* and the plane shook. Lindbergh put his hand out the window and felt sleet. He pointed his flashlight outside and saw that the wings were covered with ice. The extra weight of the ice could cause the plane to crash. He had to act quickly.

Lindbergh turned the plane around and flew out

of the cloud. The ice on the wings melted, and the plane stopped shaking. But now he was headed in the wrong direction. He turned the plane again and slowly flew around the cloud.

As he flew, Lindbergh had to avoid more clouds. He flew above them and below them. Dodging the clouds became like a game, and the challenge helped keep him awake.

During his hours in the air, Lindbergh kept a journal. He recorded his thoughts and concerns. One of his main worries was lack of sleep. Flying alone across the ocean, Lindbergh fought to stay awake. He wrote, "I will *force* my body to remain alert. I will *force* my mind to concentrate . . . I simply can't think of sleep."

After twenty hours, Lindbergh wondered how far he had gone. Was he halfway to Paris? The ocean stretched out before him, and he had no idea how much longer the trip would be. His muscles were stiff, and he felt cramped in the small cockpit. But he willed himself to continue.

Then, after twenty-seven hours, he saw something on the water. Small black specks were bobbing up and down. As he got closer, he realized they were fishing boats. Boats meant that a harbor was nearby.

He was almost at the European coastline, and Lindbergh knew the worst was over.

He flew over England and continued to France. Along the way, he ate a sandwich he had brought along and drank some water. But his thoughts were not on hunger or exhaustion. They were on landing safely and completing a successful flight.

After thirty-three hours in the air, Lindbergh was flying over France. He wrote, "I'm still at four thousand feet when I see it. That scarcely perceptible glow, as though the moon had rushed ahead of schedule. Paris is rising over the edge of the earth. . . ."

And finally, after 3,600 miles (5,792 km) and 33 1/2 hours, Lindbergh landed at Le Bourget Airport. It was 10:21 P.M. (Paris time) on May 21. Lucky Lindy had crossed the Atlantic.

HAILED AS
A HERO

AS LINDBERGH FLEW toward Paris, people throughout the world listened to news of the trip. His progress was part of every news broadcast. And as he approached France, people on the ground saw his plane and cheered.

By the time Lindbergh landed, he was already a hero. On the runway, thousands of people ran to his plane, shouting his name. He felt his plane shake and he heard wood cracking. People were taking parts of his plane as souvenirs! The attention was over-

Crowds at Le Bourget Airport in Paris. Lindbergh was surprised by the number of people who came to greet him.

whelming, even frightening. Lindbergh looked at the crowd and wondered what would happen next.

In the Spotlight

He climbed out of the cockpit, and the crowd surrounded him. Suddenly, he was lifted up in the air and carried around the runway. Lindbergh was baffled by the excitement. As he had circled the airport, he had seen thousands of headlights. He had not realized that what he was seeing was a traffic jam around the airport.

Soon two French pilots came to help him, and police surrounded the plane. Lindbergh was concerned about the safety of his plane, so it was taken to an airport hangar and guarded. Then the French pilots took Lindbergh to meet the U.S. ambassador to France. They had to drive along back roads, because the main roads in Paris were packed with people hoping to see the young flier.

Once at the U.S. Embassy in Paris, Lindbergh slept for ten hours. He was exhausted from the flight and from all the attention. But the next morning, the attention continued. He had not planned on being in the spotlight and had to borrow a suit to wear. The sleeves and pants legs were too short for the tall, lanky young man, but the crowd didn't notice. They cheered as he and the ambassador greeted them, and they asked Lucky Lindy all kinds of questions.

After spending time in France, Lindbergh then went on to Belgium and England. At each stop, he was met by royalty. He was given medals and gifts and treated to elaborate dinners and receptions.

Back in the United States

Lindbergh had planned to fly around the world. But President Calvin Coolidge wanted to bring him and

President Calvin Coolidge presenting Lindbergh with the Distinguished Flying Cross. Millions listened to the ceremony by radio.

Evangeline Lindbergh with her son, Charles, in front of the Spirit of St. Louis. *The pilot's father had died before the famous flight.*

the *Spirit of St. Louis* home by ship. Lindbergh agreed to the request. So on June 11, the USS *Monitor*, carrying Lindbergh as its special passenger, sailed up the Potomac River and into Washington, D.C. His mother joined him there (his father had died before the historic flight), and both of them were treated as guests of the president. Lindbergh was driven down Pennsylvania Avenue and a ceremony was held in front of the Washington Monument. Thousands gathered to watch, and millions listened by radio as President Coolidge welcomed him home and presented him with the Distinguished Flying Cross.

Lindbergh's next stop was New York City. There he was honored with a ticker-tape parade up Broadway. Four and a half million people lined the streets for that parade, which is still the largest in New York City history.

Lindbergh received millions of letters. Streets, babies, and even a sandwich were named for him. The American people could not get enough of this modest young man. He was named *Time* magazine's first Man of the Year.

Because of his fame, Lindbergh was offered thousands of dollars to endorse products—cigarettes, clothing, hats, and shaving cream. But he believed

Lindbergh riding in a car (above) with the New York City mayor and other dignitaries. An estimated four and a half million people watched the parade.

Lindbergh was suddenly famous. Reporters sought him out for stories, and companies tried to gain his support for their products.

he could do advertisements only for products he actually used on his trip. To him, it would be dishonest to endorse others. Even so, he earned hundreds of thousands of dollars.

Newspaper reporters asked him about his trip and his life. Lindbergh was happy to talk about aviation. He explained about his historic flight: "I believe it is the forerunner of a great air service from America to France, America to Europe, to bring our peoples nearer together in understanding and in friendship than they have ever been."

As reporters asked more personal questions, he vowed to keep his own life private. Unfortunately, this would be difficult in the years ahead.

Promoting Aviation

During the summer of 1927, Lindbergh began a three-month tour of the United States. He wanted to show how safe and reliable flying could be. Harry Guggenheim, a millionaire and former U.S. Navy pilot, helped Lindbergh with the tour. The Guggenheim Fund, which was created to promote flying, provided most of the money needed.

Lindbergh visited all of the forty-eight states. He flew 22,340 miles (35,945 km) and gave 147 speeches. His efforts did much to increase awareness of aviation. Suddenly, people came to think that flying was not so unusual. An estimated 30 million people saw Lindbergh on his cross-country tour. Undoubtedly, they were inspired by his accomplishments and hopes for the future.

Lindbergh did have high hopes for aviation, yet

Harry Guggenheim (right) accompanied Lindbergh on some of his promotional flights. The millionaire also paid for much of the three-month tour.

he felt a hesitation as well. He once wrote, "Possibly everyone will travel by air in another fifty years. I'm not sure I like the idea of millions of planes flying around overhead. I love the sky's unbroken solitude. I don't like to think of it cluttered up by aircraft, as roads are cluttered up by cars." One can only wonder what he would think of today's crowded airports and busy runways.

Meeting Anne Morrow

In December 1927, Lindbergh did a favor for Dwight Morrow, the U.S. ambassador to Mexico. Morrow was concerned about the bad relations that existed between the United States and Mexico. He hoped that a visit from Lindbergh would please the people of Mexico and improve their feelings toward the United States. So, with that goal in mind, Lindbergh flew nonstop from Washington, D.C., to Mexico City. At one point, Lindbergh encountered bad weather and flew off course. Those on the ground worried that something had happened to him, but he arrived safely—though two hours late—and greeted the large crowd waiting for him.

Lindbergh's flight to Mexico City turned out to have personal importance as well. While staying with Ambassador Morrow's family, Lindbergh met the ambassador's daughter Anne. She was twenty-one years old and a student at Smith College in Massachusetts. At the time of Lindbergh's arrival, she was visiting her family for the Christmas holidays.

The young, handsome hero of the skies had never really dated. Flying had always been his first priority. Nevertheless, he had always felt that he would like to marry and have children. So meeting Anne was a welcome event.

Initially, he was introduced to Morrow's older daughter, Elisabeth. The press even reported a romance between the two. But Lindbergh could not get Anne off his mind, so he found a way to meet her again. Months later, he telephoned her while she was staying at her family's home in New Jersey. She agreed to a first date, which turned out to be a flight over Long Island.

Lindbergh found Anne to be an intelligent and curious young woman. She was not only interested in his flying, she also wanted to learn to be a pilot herself. Before long, the two were engaged. And on May 27, 1929, Charles Lindbergh and Anne Morrow were married.

Anne Morrow Lindbergh in 1932. Charles Lindbergh appreciated his wife's intelligence and serious nature.

Spouses and Copilots

Mrs. Charles Lindbergh quickly became a part of her husband's life in aviation. She traveled with him and appeared at air shows. She also assisted him in his work for Transcontinental Air Transport, which later became Pan American World Airways (Pan Am).

The Lindberghs enjoyed working together, but their personal life was difficult. They fooled the press and kept their wedding a secret. And they avoided reporters during their honeymoon. But once married, the young couple could not escape the media. Wherever they went, reporters and photographers followed, hoping for a quote or a photograph. The Lindberghs quickly grew to dislike the lack of privacy.

Charles began giving Anne flying lessons a few months after their marriage. He was a very strict teacher, but Anne didn't mind. She wanted to learn all that she could. In addition to flying, Anne learned about navigation. Soon she was Charles's radio operator, navigator, and copilot.

On a flight from Los Angeles to New York on Easter Sunday, 1930, the Lindberghs set a speed record. They made the trip in a Lockheed Sirius plane and completed it in fourteen hours and forty

Charles and Anne Lindbergh in front of their plane on Easter Sunday in 1930. They set a speed record from Los Angeles to New York.

minutes. The flight was a success, but the last four hours were difficult for Anne. She was seven months pregnant at the time, and she got very sick in the air. But she never complained. She did not want to spoil the special flight for her husband.

Becoming a Father

About two months later, on June 22, Anne gave birth to a son. The couple tried to shield Charles Jr. from the press, but the public clamored to know about

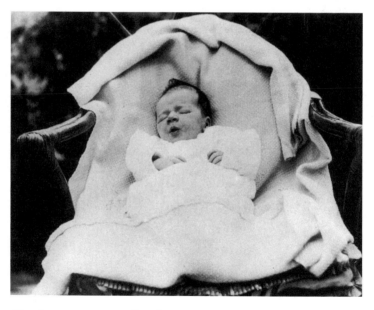

Charles Augustus Lindbergh Jr. at two weeks of age. This little boy was famous from the moment he was born.

the baby. Lindbergh tried to concentrate on flying. He wanted to keep his professional life separate from his personal one.

But the press would not allow the Lindberghs their privacy. Everywhere the aviators went, light-bulbs flashed and reporters followed. Even from its beginning, the life of the Lindberghs' first son was a media spectacle. And with the events that were soon to follow, the attention from the press would only heighten.

FACING DIFFICULT TIMES

AFTER THE BIRTH of Charlie, as Anne called him, the Lindberghs decided to build a house near Hopewell, New Jersey. They enjoyed the area's country atmosphere but also liked how close it was to New York City.

Lindbergh continued to work for Pan Am. Serving as consultant, he and Anne planned a flight to the Far East. They wanted to explore air routes to Alaska, Japan, and China. It was a big project and the longest trip they had ever made together. Because they were going to be away for several months, they decided that Charlie would stay with Anne's mother, Betty Morrow.

To the Far East

In July 1931, the Lindberghs set out in the Lockheed Sirius they used on their previous flight from Los Angeles to New York. Their first destination was Canada, which had very few airports in 1931. They equipped their plane with pontoons so that they could land on water if necessary.

From Canada, they headed to Alaska and continued over the Bering Sea and to Japan and China. They arrived in China shortly after the Yangtze River had flooded. People all along the river needed food and medical supplies. Seeing the difficult situation, the Lindberghs volunteered for China's National Flood Relief Commission. They flew much-needed supplies to the area. They visited hospitals and were greeted with gratitude by the Chinese people.

They were eager to go on to the Chinese capital of Beijing, but then they received the news that Anne's father had died of a stroke. They canceled the rest of the trip and returned home as quickly as possible.

The Lindberghs visiting a hospital in Tokyo in 1931. They also spent time in China that year.

Family Tragedy

In late February 1932, the Lindberghs spent a typical weekend at their home in Hopewell. They intended to leave Monday morning to spend the week with the Morrows in Englewood. Upon seeing that Charlie had a cold, however, they decided to stay for a few days longer.

On the evening of March 1, 1932—a cold and rainy night—Charlie's nanny, Betty Gow, checked on the sleeping baby in his nursery. All was well. About an hour later, Lindbergh later remembered

A ladder leading up to the window from which Charlie Lindbergh was kidnapped. His nursery was on the second story of the Hopewell house.

WANTED

INFORMATION AS TO THE WHEREABOUTS OF

CHAS. A. LINDBERGH, JR.

OF HOPEWELL, N. J.

SON OF COL. CHAS. A. LINDBERGH

World-Famous Aviator

This child was kidnaped from his home in Hopewell, N. J., between 8 and 10 p. m. on Tuesday, March 1, 1932.

DESCRIPTION:

Age, 20 months	Hair, blond, curly
Weight, 27 to 30 lbs.	Eyes, dark blue
Height, 29 inches	Complexion, light

Deep dimple in center of chin
Dressed in one-piece coverall night suit

ADDRESS ALL COMMUNICATIONS TO
COL. H. N. SCHWARZKOPF, TRENTON, N. J., or
COL. CHAS. A. LINDBERGH, HOPEWELL, N. J.

ALL COMMUNICATIONS WILL BE TREATED IN CONFIDENCE

March 11, 1932

COL. H. NORMAN SCHWARZKOPF
Supt. New Jersey State Police, Trenton, N. J.

A poster asking for information about the Lindbergh kidnapping. Unfortunately, few details were ever known.

hearing a noise, perhaps that of a crate falling. But, considering the high winds that were blowing outside, he gave the strange noise little thought. After another hour passed, Betty Gow checked on Charlie again, but this time all was not well. The crib was empty and the twenty-month-old infant was gone. Charles A. Lindbergh Jr. had been kidnapped!

The police were immediately called in, and a search began. Footprints were found outside in the wet earth. Below the nursery window were two small holes in the ground, probably made by the broken ladder that was found nearby. And fresh tire tracks were spotted in the dirt road that led to the house.

In the nursery, a ransom note was discovered. It was filled with misspelled words and was hard to read. But its meaning was clear. The Lindberghs would be contacted in two to four days. And the kidnapper requested $50,000 for the return of the baby.

The Crime of the Century

Within only a few hours, reporters swarmed the Hopewell property. Complete strangers filled the yard and looked through the windows. Not even in

The ransom note found in Charlie's nursery the night he disappeared. Another demand was mailed to the Lindberghs.

the face of this crisis were the Lindberghs allowed any privacy.

Lindbergh felt strongly that they should do whatever the kidnapper asked. All he wanted was for Charlie to be returned safely. In the meantime, the police considered several theories. One possibility was that the kidnapper was someone who worked for the Lindberghs, because few people knew they would be at the Hopewell house on that night. But no hard evidence linking an employee to the crime was ever discovered.

As the story of the kidnapping hit the papers, the media dubbed the event "the crime of the century." People from all over the United States and all over the world offered advice and sympathy. A few days later, another ransom note was mailed to the Lindberghs. This one told them they should not have involved the police, and it demanded an additional $20,000.

Before long, a man named John F. Condon offered to act as go-between for Lindbergh and the kidnapper. Condon idolized the young pilot and wanted to help in any way he could. Both Lindbergh and the kidnapper agreed that Condon could be involved.

An Unbearable Loss

One dark night, Condon and Lindbergh followed the kidnapper's instructions and took the money to Woodlawn Cemetery. They were given a note stating that the baby was all right and telling where he was to be found. But the note turned out to be untrue.

On May 12, 1932—about ten weeks after he disappeared—the body of little Charlie was discovered. It was in the woods less than 4 miles (6.4 km) from the house in Hopewell. It is now believed that the baby died on the very night he was taken and that all the kidnapper's demands were lies.

In 1934, a man was arrested for the crime. He was a carpenter named Bruno Richard Hauptmann. He was suspected because he had been using money that matched the bills used in the Lindbergh ransom. The rest of the evidence against him was weak, but he was convicted of kidnapping and murder in 1935. The following year, he was sentenced to death.

In the time that has passed since the kidnapping, a number of theories have been considered. Many believe that Hauptmann was innocent but police felt pressured to blame someone and close the case.

Reporters and spectators at the site where Charles Lindbergh Jr.'s body was found. After ten weeks, the search was over.

Others feel that Hauptmann was accused because he was a German immigrant. Some believe that a maid or butler was guilty of the crime, and others have even considered Anne Morrow Lindbergh's sister Elisabeth. There is another theory that John

Condon, the seemingly helpful go-between, played a part in the crime. The truth behind this mystery may never be known.

What is known is how terrible the loss was for Charlie's parents.

The Lindberghs had always hated attention from the media, and ultimately they blamed their fame for the loss of their son. They went on to have three other sons and two daughters. But losing Charlie made the Lindberghs even more private and more suspicious of the public than ever.

A New Law

Perhaps the only positive result of the Lindbergh kidnapping was the creation of a new law. Congress passed the "Lindbergh law," which made kidnapping a federal crime in two instances: if the victim is taken across state lines or if the mail service is used to deliver ransom demands. In the Lindbergh case, the baby never left New Jersey; however, a ransom note was mailed to the Lindbergh home.

Back in the Air

In the summer of 1933, Charles and Anne boarded their Lockheed Sirius and took off into the skies again. They flew to Greenland, Denmark, Sweden, and Finland. The purpose of this European tour was to scout air routes for Pan Am. They made stops in Leningrad and Moscow, and flew on to England, Holland, Switzerland, Spain, and Portugal. Then they headed for South America.

By this time, they had been gone for five months. Anne was eager to get home, but Charles was happy to continue traveling. Up in the clouds, he was free from the media attention that had plagued him for years. He didn't have to answer questions or dodge photographers. He could just fly and be left alone. But he couldn't stay away forever, and by Christmas 1933, the two returned home.

Causing Controversy

Lindbergh never hesitated to speak his mind. Sometimes, his opinions caused trouble. In 1934, President Franklin D. Roosevelt decided that the delivery of airmail should no longer be handled by the commercial airlines. He wanted the U.S. Army Air Corps to take over the responsibility. His decision was based on the report that the largest companies got the airmail contracts, even though they charged more money than the smaller companies. The contracts should have

President Franklin D. Roosevelt believed that airmail should be delivered by the U.S. Army Corps. Lindbergh publicly disagreed with him.

gone to the lowest bidders, but a congressional study showed that the more powerful companies used political influence to get the contracts.

Lindbergh knew the presidents of many of these large airlines. Perhaps he put too much trust in these businessmen, but he could not believe they would do anything wrong. Nevertheless, these feelings of trust may have been naïve on Lindbergh's part. Also, Lindbergh feared that the pilots of the U.S. Army Air Corps might not have the experience needed to deliver airmail. He worried that pilots not accustomed to flying at night would be at risk. So he opposed the president's decision, and his opposition was embarrassing for President Franklin D. Roosevelt.

Lindbergh was right about the pilots' lack of experience. Several pilots crashed. Some were killed, and others were badly injured. The public supported Lindbergh's opinion. Soon President Roosevelt was forced to change his mind and return the contracts to the large airline companies.

Lindbergh was pleased with the decision, but he did not realize how the controversy had affected the president. Roosevelt was not happy with this apparent defeat, and he would not forget what Lindbergh had done.

To England, Germany, and the Soviet Union

In 1935, a few weeks before Charlie's accused kidnapper was to be executed, Charles and Anne went to England hoping to escape the press. Their second son, Jon, had been born, and they wished to lead a more quiet life.

The Lindberghs with their second son, Jon, arriving in England. They left the United States before Bruno Richard Hauptmann was executed.

The next year, Lindbergh received an invitation to visit Germany. Adolf Hitler and the Nazi Party had come to power in 1933, and Hermann Göring, the head of German aviation, wanted Lindbergh to see the projects the Nazis were working on.

Both Charles and Anne agreed to go to Germany, and they arrived just before the 1936 Olympic

Adolf Hitler (left) with Hermann Göring. Lindbergh came to know both of these men during his visits to Germany.

Games in Berlin. They sat with General Göring at the Olympics and were applauded by the crowd. All around them, they saw the Olympic flags along with the red-and-black Nazi flags marked with swastikas. The swastika was the symbol of the Nazi Party, which believed that the white race was superior to all other people.

The aircraft factories he saw in Germany impressed Lindbergh. He felt the Germans had made great progress in aviation, and he respected the German people. Though he knew a second world war was likely in the near future, he had high regard for Adolf Hitler and found him to be efficient and often times inspiring.

In the fall of 1937, Lindbergh visited Germany again. He inspected several new airplanes and even flew one of their bombers. After this tour, Lindbergh wrote a memorandum to the U.S. military in which he described the strengths of the German aviation program. U.S. government leaders found Lindbergh's insights to be important, and they asked him to meet with them in Washington, D.C.

Charles and Anne then spent three months in the United States. Charles gave the U.S. government the information it requested. The government then asked Lindbergh to provide the same kind of information on aviation in the Soviet Union. So in 1938, the Lindberghs traveled to Moscow. There they were entertained and treated well. But they noted that life in the Soviet Union was difficult. Joseph Stalin, the Soviet leader, headed a controlling government that made many citizens fear for their lives.

Lindbergh returned to Germany later that year and attended a ceremony in Berlin. There he was honored with the Service Cross of the German Eagle. This medal was created to honor foreigners who had served Germany in some way. Lindbergh was surprised and embarrassed by the honor. Anne worried that the award would send the wrong message about her husband and his relationship with the German government. She had good reason to worry.

Soon after Lindbergh received the award, violence erupted in Germany. On November 9, 1938, a night later called *Kristallnacht*, the Nazis attacked many Jewish people, destroying their businesses and smashing their synagogues. They beat thousands of Jewish people and took between 20,000 and 30,000 Jews to concentration camps.

Many U.S. citizens feared Adolf Hitler. Public opinion was that the Lindberghs' trips to Germany

The day after Kristallnacht *in Berlin. Nazi troops attacked many Jewish people and destroyed their businesses and synagogues.*

and his association with Hitler were inappropriate. Many people questioned the medal the Nazis had given Lindbergh and called for him to return it. Nevertheless, Lindbergh continued to respect the German people and saw no reason to return the Service Cross of the German Eagle.

Approaching World War II

While Lindbergh was in Europe, General Henry Arnold asked him to return to the United States. Leaders around the world knew that a war might be on the horizon. General Arnold hoped Lindbergh would lend his expertise and help him assess U.S. air power. He wanted the U.S. military to be ready for whatever was coming.

During the spring and summer of 1939, Lindbergh traveled throughout the United States. Serving as a colonel in the U.S. Army Corps Reserve, he inspected aircraft factories and aviation-research centers. He was happy to lend his knowledge to the buildup of U.S. aircraft. However, Lindbergh strongly felt that the United States should stay out of any conflict brewing in Europe. He believed that Germany was quite capable and could easily defeat Britain and France. Some Americans, called isolationists, shared this belief.

Lindbergh soon resigned his commission in the U.S. Army so that he could speak his mind more freely. He made nationwide radio addresses. In these speeches, he urged the American people to stay out of the conflict in Europe. He also wrote articles and spoke at rallies, and all of his appearances received media attention. President Roosevelt, of course, opposed his views.

Turning Points

As World War II (1939–1945) progressed, it became clear that Britain was stronger than Lindbergh had reported. Inspired by Prime Minister Winston Churchill, the British stood their ground alone against the Germans. Many Americans were beginning to feel that the British deserved U.S. support.

At one point, a group of isolationists called America First approached Lindbergh. This group was comprised of prominent Americans who wished to stay out of World War II. Their members included pacifists, as well as American Nazis. Lindbergh joined America First and traveled throughout the United States giving speeches for the group.

In September 1941, while in Des Moines, Iowa, he gave a speech that disturbed many Americans. In it he stated, "The three most important groups who have been pressing this country toward war are the British, the Jewish, and the Roosevelt Administration . . . the major war agitators in this country. . . . Most of the Jewish interests in the country are behind the war, and they control a

Charles Lindbergh speaking at an America First rally. The group believed that the United States should not get involved in World War II.

huge part of our press and radio and most of our motion pictures."

Lindbergh's words were controversial to say the least. Many began to feel he opposed the war because he disliked the Jewish people. Some America First members resigned after this speech, while others tried to keep their distance from Lindbergh.

The United States at War

On December 7, 1941, Japan launched a surprise air attack on a U.S. Navy base in Pearl Harbor, Hawaii. More than 2,000 Americans were killed in that attack. Almost immediately, the United States declared war on Japan, an ally of Germany and Italy.

Once the United States was fully involved in the war, Lindbergh felt it was his duty to serve. America First had disbanded, and the American people stood behind President Roosevelt and the armed forces. Lindbergh's request to be reinstated in the military was denied, however. President Roosevelt made it clear that Charles Lindbergh was not to be a part of the U.S. effort in World War II. The once-heralded, famous pilot had fallen out of favor because of his admiration for Nazi Germany and his controversial statements about Jewish people.

A LIFE'S
ACHIEVEMENTS

I N SPITE OF President Roosevelt's ruling against him, Lindbergh made a contribution during World War II. First, he worked as a consultant to Henry Ford, the car manufacturer. Ford produced airplanes during the war, and Lindbergh helped solve many production problems at the Ford factory. He also was a consultant for the United Aircraft Corporation.

But he was eager to get back in the air. The pilot in him was tired of giving speeches and offering opinions. He wanted to fly planes. Some people in power still saw

Lindbergh as a hero, no matter what he had said about the Germans and the Jews. So they gave him the title of "civilian observer," and they allowed him to fly several test-pilot missions. He offered advice to younger pilots and gave talks about such issues as the conservation of gasoline during flight.

After the War

In the years after World War II, Lindbergh was not seen as the hero he once was. His views prior to the war had tarnished his reputation. But many people still sought him out for his knowledge about aviation. He served as technical consultant for the U.S. Air Force and continued to work for Pan Am.

Lindbergh also proved his talents as an author. In 1953, he published *The Spirit of St. Louis*, a book that told about his childhood as well as his historic flight across the Atlantic. This book was a best-seller and was praised by literary critics. It won the Pulitzer Prize in 1954.

Lindbergh was also reinstated in the military reserves in 1954. President Dwight Eisenhower recognized the contributions Lindbergh had made during the war and promoted him to brigadier general.

Family Life

Throughout his years as a pilot, Lindbergh was often away from home. The work that he loved required that he travel a great deal. He loved these adventures, though they kept him from his family.

Even after his fame had lessened and Lindbergh could have been home more often, he always seemed to have a new project to work on. On some days, he spent much time with his children. But at other times, he was completely unavailable. Anne put it well: "You know Charles, he'll be here when he's here."

Friend of the Environment

During his many hours in the air, Charles Lindbergh developed a healthy respect for the natural world. He realized that human activity was destroying many parts of the environment. From his airplane, he saw areas of green devoured by housing and forests stripped for their lumber. He saw polluted rivers and littered highways.

Lindbergh became a supporter of the World Wildlife Fund during the 1960s. He traveled from country to country and worked to save endangered species of animals. As a boy on his family's farm, he

Lindbergh in 1968 while attending a wildlife conference in Rio de Janeiro, Brazil. Environmental causes became important to him later in his life.

had always enjoyed nature. As a grown man, he felt a duty to help preserve that natural world.

In 1971, Lindbergh traveled to the Philippines and visited with the Tasaday tribe. This group of people still lived a primitive existence. They had no weapons or modern tools or machines. They lived in caves and survived on fruit, small animals, and roots. Because of Lindbergh's efforts on their behalf, the tribe was allowed to remain as they were. The Philippine government protected their land and their lifestyle.

Wearing a hat presented to him by a tribe in the Philippines. Lindbergh worked to protect the tribe's existence.

Endings

Always a man full of energy, Lindbergh was surprised when he suddenly began feeling tired. He canceled a few trips and tried to take it easy, but he continued not to feel well. Before long, he was diagnosed with cancer.

Lindbergh decided to spend his last days in Hawaii, in a cottage he had bought on Maui. He carefully planned his funeral, tending to the details as he did with all the other projects he had always embraced. On August 26, 1974, Lucky Lindy's long life ended.

Being Remembered

While writing about his historic flight to Paris, Charles Lindbergh once asked, "Why does one want to walk on wings? Why should man want to fly at all? People often ask those questions. But what civilization was not founded on adventure, and how long could one exist without it?" Undoubtedly, Lindbergh embraced the adventure that was, for him, such a part of life. And through his flights, people around the world tasted a bit of that adventure as well.

In the years since his death, he has been remembered in many ways. Some remember the

The grave of Charles A. Lindbergh in Maui. He died on this
Hawaiian island on August 26, 1974.

happy young man who flew to Paris. And others remember a frightened father pleading for the safe return of his infant son. Still others remember an apparent Nazi sympathizer. And some others remember a man who did important work for the natural world he loved.

The Spirit of St. Louis *on display at the Smithsonian Institution in Washington, D.C. Visitors can see a very real part of aviation history.*

No doubt, Lindbergh was not the perfect hero the American people first perceived him to be. He did not react well to being in the public eye. He may very well have been a victim of Adolf Hitler's strong influence. And he was by no means the ultimate husband and father. But he was a brave and most remarkable pilot—a man who made an important mark in the history of aviation.

TIMELINE

1902	Charles Lindbergh born in Detroit, Michigan, on February 4
1920	Starts college at the University of Wisconsin in September
1922	Leaves school and enrolls in a flying school in Lincoln, Nebraska, in March; in April, goes up in a plane for the first time; during the summer and fall, works as a wing walker, parachute jumper, and mechanic
1923	Buys his own plane in April and flies his first solo flight; barnstorms on his own that summer
1924	Enters the Army Air Service training school in San Antonio, Texas, in March
1926	Becomes an airmail pilot and flies the route from St. Louis to Chicago, in April; begins to consider the flight from New York to Paris
1927	Oversees the building of the *Spirit of St. Louis*; in May, flies the plane from San Diego to Long

Island, New York; May 20–21, flies the plane non-stop from Roosevelt Field to Le Bourget Field in Paris; returns home in June and receives the Distinguished Flying Cross; tours the United States with the *Spirit of St. Louis* to promote the idea of flying; meets Anne Morrow in December

1929	Marries Anne Morrow on May 27
1930	With Anne, breaks the speed record for flight from Los Angeles to New York; a son, Charles Jr., is born on June 22.
1931	Explores air routes for Pan American World Airways (Pan Am) in Alaska, Japan, and China
1932	Young Charles is kidnapped, a ransom is paid, but the boy is found dead; another son, Jon, is born on August 16.
1933	Scouts out more air routes for Pan Am
1936	The kidnapper of son Charles is found guilty and sentenced to die; Lindbergh visits Nazi Germany.
1937	Son Land is born on May 12; visits Germany again
1938	Visits Moscow; visits Germany and receives the Service Cross of the German Eagle
1939	Speaks out against U.S. involvement in World War II (1939–1945)
1940	Daughter Anne born on October 2
1941	Joins a group called America First, which opposes U.S. involvement in the war; after the

	United States enters World War II, volunteers his services in the Air Corps but is rejected because of his views
1941–45	Serves as a consultant to aircraft companies; tours the South Pacific and Germany after the war
1942	Son Scott born on August 13
1946	Daughter Reeve born on October 20
1954	His book *The Spirit of St. Louis* wins the Pulitzer Prize; his military status is restored by President Eisenhower and he is promoted to brigadier general, in April.
1960s	Supports wildlife conservation
1971	Visits the Tasaday tribe in the Philippines
1974	Dies in Maui on August 26

HOW TO BECOME A PILOT

The Job

The best-known pilots are the commercial airline pilots who fly for the airlines. Responsible, skilled professionals, pilots are among the highest paid workers in the United States. The typical flight-deck crew includes the captain, who is the pilot in command, and the copilot, or first officer. In larger aircraft, there may be a third member of the crew, called the flight engineer (or second officer). The captain is in complete command of the crew, the aircraft, and the passengers or cargo while the plane is in flight. In the air, the captain also has the force of law. The aircraft may hold 30 people or 300, or be completely loaded with freight, depending on the airline and type of operations. The plane may be fitted with turbojet engines, turboprop engines (which have propellers driven by jet engines), or propeller engines. An aircraft may operate near the speed of sound and at altitudes as high as 40,000 feet (12,200 m).

In addition to flying the aircraft, pilots must perform safety-related tasks. Before each flight, they check weather and flight conditions, make sure that enough fuel is on board, and review the maintenance status of the aircraft. The captain briefs all crew members, including the flight attendants, about the flight. Pilots must also perform checks to test the instruments, controls, and electronic and mechanical systems on the flight deck. Pilots coordinate their flight plan with airplane dispatchers and air-traffic controllers. Flight plans include information about the airplane, the passenger or cargo load, and the route the pilot is planning to take.

Once all preflight duties have been performed, the captain taxis the aircraft to the runway and prepares for takeoff. Takeoff speeds are based on the aircraft's weight. All the aircraft's systems, levers, and switches must be in proper position for takeoff. After takeoff, the pilots may turn on an electrical device known as the autopilot. This device can be programmed to keep the plane on desired course and at a specific altitude. With or without the aid of the autopilot, pilots must constantly monitor the aircraft's instruments.

Because pilots may encounter turbulence, emergencies, and other hazardous situations during a flight, good judgment is extremely important. Pilots also receive continuous training and evaluation on their handling of in-flight emergencies as well as their operation of the aircraft during difficult weather conditions.

During a flight, pilots monitor aircraft systems, keep a watchful eye on local weather conditions, perform checklists, and maintain constant communication with air-traffic controllers along the flight route. The busiest times for pilots are during takeoff and landing. The weather conditions at the aircraft's destination must be obtained and analyzed. The aircraft must be maneuvered and properly configured to make a landing on the runway. When the clouds are low and visibility is poor, pilots must rely on the instruments. These instruments include an altimeter and an artificial horizon. Pilots select the radio navigation frequencies and corresponding course for the ground-based radio and microwave signals that provide horizontal, and in some cases vertical, guidance to the landing runway.

After the pilots have safely landed the aircraft, the captain taxis it to the ramp or gate area where passengers leave the plane and cargo is removed. Pilots then follow "after landing and shutdown" checklist procedures. They also inform maintenance crews of any problems noticed during the flight.

Pilots must keep detailed logs of their flight hours, both for payroll purposes and to comply with Federal Aviation Administration (FAA) regulations. Pilots with major airlines generally have few nonflying duties. Pilots with smaller airlines, charter services, and other air service companies may be responsible for loading the aircraft, refueling, keeping records, performing minor repairs and maintenance, and arranging for major repairs.

The chief pilot directs the operation of the airline's flight department. This individual is in charge of training new pilots, preparing their schedules and assigning flight personnel, reviewing their performance, and improving their morale and efficiency. Chief pilots make sure that all the regulations affecting flight operations are observed. They also advise the airline during contract negotiations with the pilots' union and handle a multitude of administrative details.

Various other types of pilots include business pilots, or executive pilots, who fly for company planes. These pilots transport cargo, products, or executives and also maintain the company's planes. Test pilots, though few in number, are very important. Combining knowledge of flying with an engineering background, they test new models of planes and make sure they function properly. Flight instructors are pilots who teach others how to fly. They may teach in classrooms or provide in-flight instruction, or both. Other pilots work as examiners, or check pilots. They may fly with experienced pilots as part of their periodic review. They may also give examinations to pilots applying for licenses.

Some pilots are employed in the following specialties: photogrammetry pilots fly planes or helicopters over designated areas and photograph the Earth's surface for mapping and other purposes. Facilities-flight-check pilots fly specially equipped planes to test air-navigational aids, air-traffic controls, and communications equipment, and evaluate installation sites for such equipment. A supervising pilot directs this testing.

Requirements
High School All future pilots must complete high school. A college-preparatory curriculum is recommended because pilots need at least some college education. Science and mathematics are two important subjects for prospective pilots. Students should also take any computer courses that may be offered. Students can start pursuing their pilot's license while still in high school.

Postsecondary Most companies employing pilots require at least two years of college; many require applicants to be college graduates. Courses in engineering, meteorology, physics, and mathematics are helpful in preparing for a pilot's career. Flying can also be learned in either military or civilian flying schools. There are approximately 1,000 FAA-certified civilian flying schools, including some colleges and universities that offer degree credit for pilot training. Pilots leaving military service are in great demand.

Licensing and Certification Rigid training requirements must be met to become a pilot. Although getting a private pilot's license is relatively simple, a commercial license may be quite difficult to obtain. Any student who is sixteen or older and who can pass the rigid mandatory physical examination may apply for permission to take flying instruction. When the training is completed, a written examination is given. If prospective pilots pass the examination, they may then apply for private pilot's licenses. To qualify, a person must be at least seventeen years of age, successfully fulfill a solo-flying requirement of twenty hours or more, and qualify in instrument flying and cross-country flying. Student pilots are not allowed to carry passengers; private pilots may carry passengers but may not accept any payment or other compensation for their services.

The FAA must license all pilots and copilots before they fly commercial aircraft. An applicant who is eighteen years old and has 250 hours of flying time can apply for a commercial airplane pilot's license. To apply for this license, a candidate must pass a rigid physical examination and a written test given by the FAA. The test covers safe flight operations, federal aviation regulations, navigation principles, radio operation, and meteorology. The applicant also must provide proof that the minimum flight-time requirements have been completed and demonstrate adequate flying skill and technical competence.

Before pilots or copilots receive an FAA license, they must receive a rating for the kind of plane they can fly—single-engine, multiengine, or seaplane—and for the specific type of plane, such as Boeing 737 or 757.

An instrument rating by the FAA and a restricted radio telephone operator's permit by the Federal Communications Commission (FCC) are also required.

All airline captains must have an air-transport pilot license. Applicants for this license must be at least twenty-three years old and have a minimum of 1,500 hours of flight time, including night flying and instrument time. All pilots are subject to flight reviews every two years, regular FAA flight checks every six months, simulator tests, and medical exams. The FAA also makes unannounced spot-check inspections of all pilots. Jet pilots, helicopter pilots, and agricultural pilots all must have special training in their respective fields.

Other Requirements   Sound physical and emotional health is essential for aspiring pilots. Emotional stability is necessary because many people depend upon a pilot remaining calm, no matter how trying the situation. Physical health is equally important. Vision and hearing must be perfect; coordination must be excellent; heart rate and blood pressure must be normal.

Exploring

High-school students who are interested in flying may join the Explorers (Boy Scouts of America) or a high-school aviation club. At sixteen, they may start taking flying lessons. One of the most valuable experiences for a high-school student who wants to become a pilot is to learn to be a ham radio operator. By so doing, they meet one of the qualifications for commercial flying.

Starting Out

A large percentage of commercial pilots have received their training in the armed forces. If application is made within a year after leaving the service, a military pilot who applies for a commercial airplane pilot's license is required to pass only the Federal Aviation Regulations examination.

Pilots with the necessary qualifications and license may apply directly to a commercial airline for a job. If accepted, they will go through a company orientation course, usually including both classroom instruction and practical training in company planes.

Those who are interested in becoming business pilots can start their careers in mechanics. They may also have military flying experience, but the strongest recommendation for a business pilot's job is an airframe and power-plant (A and P) rating. They should also have at least 500 hours of flying time and have both commercial and instrument ratings on their licenses. They apply directly to the firm for which they would like to work.

Advancement

Many beginning pilots start out as copilots. Seniority is a pilot's most important asset. If pilots leave one employer to work for another, they must start over again, no matter how much experience was gained with the first employer. The position of captain on a large airline is a high-seniority, high-prestige, and high-paying job. Pilots may also advance to the position of check pilot, testing other pilots for advanced ratings; chief pilot, supervising the work of other pilots; or to administrative or executive positions (ground operations) with a commercial airline. They may also become self-employed by starting a flying business, such as a flight instruction school, agricultural aviation, air-taxi, or charter service.

Work Environment

Airline pilots work with the best possible equipment and under highly favorable circumstances. They command a great deal of respect. Although many pilots regularly fly the same routes, no two flights are ever the same. FAA regulations limit airline pilots to no more than 100 flying hours per month, and most work around 75 hours per month, with few nonflying duties. This is because a pilot's job can be extremely stressful.

During flights, they must maintain constant concentration on a variety of factors. They must always be alert to changes in conditions and to any problems that may occur. They are often responsible for hundreds of lives besides their own, and they are always aware that flying contains an element of risk. During emergencies, they must react quickly, logically, and decisively. Pilots often work irregular hours. They may be away from home a lot and are subject to jet lag and other conditions associated with flying. Pilots employed with smaller airlines may also be required to perform other, nonflying duties, which increase the number of hours they work each month. For pilots who handle small planes, emergency equipment, and supply routes to remote and isolated areas, the hazards may be more evident. Dropping medical supplies in Somalia, flying relief supplies into war zones, or delivering mail to northern Alaska are more difficult tasks than most pilots face. Business-pilot schedules may be highly irregular, and these pilots are on call for a great portion of their off-duty time. Business pilots and most private and small-plane pilots are also frequently called upon to perform maintenance and repairs.

Employers

Commercial airlines, including both passenger and cargo-transport companies, are the largest employers of pilots. Pilots also work in general aviation, and many are trained and employed by the military.

Earnings

Airline pilots are among the highest paid workers in the country. The 1998 average starting salary for airline pilots was about $15,000 at small turboprop airlines and $26,500 at larger, major airlines. Pilots with six years of experience made $28,000 a year at turboprop airlines and nearly $76,800 at the largest airlines. Senior captains on the largest aircraft earned as much as $200,000 a year. Salaries vary widely depending on a number of factors, including the specific airline, type of aircraft flown, number of years with a company, and level of experience. Airline pilots are also paid more for international and nighttime flights. A survey conducted by *Rotor & Wing* magazine reports that helicopter pilots who worked for corporations earned $54,601 in 1999, while commercial helicopter pilots earned $42,154.

Pilots with the airlines receive life and health insurance and retirement benefits; if they fail their FAA physical exam during their career, they are eligible to receive disability benefits. Some airlines give pilots allowances for buying and cleaning their uniforms. Pilots and their families may usually fly free or at reduced fares on their own or other airlines.

Outlook

The U.S. Department of Labor predicts that employment for pilots will grow more slowly than the average for all other occupations through the year 2008. The recent restructuring of the airline industry and budget reductions in the U.S. military have forced many pilots to retire and enter the civilian workforce. Additionally, the number of people interested in this career has increased due to the appealing combination of high pay, prestige, and travel benefits.

The airline industry expects passenger travel to grow by as much as 60 percent, but this expansion will largely be offset by the use of computerized flight-management systems (which will eliminate many flight-engineer positions) and the use of larger planes, which will reduce the need for new pilots.

Employment for business pilots will also grow more slowly than the average. The recession of the early 1990s caused a decrease in the numbers of business and executive flights as more companies chose to fly with smaller and regional airlines rather than buy and operate their own planes. Helicopter pilots, on the other hand, will enjoy stronger employment growth as police, fire, and rescue departments increasingly rely on their services.

The aviation industry remains extremely sensitive to changes in the economy. When an economic downswing causes a decline in air travel, airline pilots may be given a furlough. Business flying, flight instruction, and testing of new aircraft are also adversely affected by recessions.

TO LEARN MORE ABOUT PILOTS

Books

Ayres, Carter M. *Pilots and Aviation.* Minneapolis: Lerner Publications, 1990.

Buchanan, Doug. *Air and Space.* Philadelphia: Chelsea House, 1999.

Greenberg, Keith Elliot. *Test Pilot: Taking Chances in the Air.* Woodbridge, Conn.: Blackbirch Press, 1997.

Rosenbaum, Roger A. *Aviators.* New York: Facts on File, 1992.

Schomp, Virginia. *If You Were a Pilot.* New York: Benchmark Books, 1999.

Taylor, Richard L. *The First Supersonic Flight.* New York: Franklin Watts, 1994.

Websites
Air Line Pilots Association, International
http://www.alpa.org/

Federal Aviation Administration
http://www.faa.gov

International Federation of Air Line Pilots Associations
http://www.ifalpa.org

National Transportation Safety Board
http://www.ntsb.gov

Where to Write
Air Line Pilots Association, International
1625 Massachusetts Avenue, N.W.
Washington, DC 20036
703/689-2270

Air Transport Association of America
1301 Pennsylvania Avenue, N.W., Suite 1100
Washington, DC 20004-1707
202/626-4000
E-mail: ata@air-transport.org

Federal Aviation Administration
800 Independence Ave, S.W.
Washington, DC 20591

Federal Aviation Administration
Flight Standards Division
Fitzgerald Federal Building
John F. Kennedy International Airport
Jamaica, NY 11430

International Federation of Air Line Pilots Associations
Interpilot House
Gogmore Lane
Chertsey, Surrey
England KT169AP

National Transportation Safety Board
490 L'Enfant Plaza, S.W.
Washington, DC 20594

TO LEARN MORE ABOUT CHARLES LINDBERGH

Books

Burkett, Molly. *Pioneers of the Air.* New York: Barrons Juvenile, 1998.

Denenberg, Barry. *An American Hero: The True Story of Charles A. Lindbergh.* New York: Scholastic, 1996.

Kent, Zachary. *Charles Lindbergh and the Spirit of St. Louis.* New York: Silver Moon Press, 1998.

Oxlade, Chris. *Flight through Time.* Austin, Tex.: Raintree/Steck Vaughn, 1996.

Stein, R. Conrad. *The Spirit of St. Louis.* Chicago: Childrens Press, 1994.

Taylor, Richard L. *The First Solo Transatlantic Flight: The Story of Charles Lindbergh and His Airplane, the Spirit of St. Louis.* New York: Franklin Watts, 1995.

Yonklin, Paula, *Spirit of St. Louis.* New York: Crestwood House, 1994.

Websites

The American Experience: Lindbergh

http://www.pbs.org/wgbh/amex/lindbergh/
A PBS-sponsored website that features information about the film *Lindbergh* as well as articles about Lindbergh's life. Includes a teacher's guide and a timeline of important dates in aviation

The Charles A. and Anne Morrow Lindbergh Foundation

http://www.mtn.org/lindfdtn/
Explains the Lindberghs' view of a balance between technological advancement and environmental preservation

The Charles A. Lindbergh House

http://www.mnhs.org./places/sites/lh/
Site for the home on the Mississippi River where Lindbergh spent boyhood summers

Two Legends of Aviation

http://www.worldbook.com/fun/aviator/html/twolegend.htm
A site sponsored by *World Book* and featuring the lives of Charles Lindbergh and Amelia Earhart

INTERESTING PLACES TO VISIT

Charles A. Lindbergh State Park
1620 Lindbergh Drive South
Little Falls, Minnesota 56345
320/632-3154
http://www.mnhs.org./places/sites/lh/
The Minnesota Historical Society has restored and maintains the boyhood home where Lindbergh spent summers.

National Air and Space Museum
7th and Independence Avenue, S.W.
Washington, D.C. 20560
202/357-1400
http://www.nasm.si.edu/
The Smithsonian Institution maintains an exhibit that features Lindbergh's plane, the *Spirit of St. Louis*.

INDEX

Page numbers in *italics* indicate illustrations.

ABOUT THE AUTHOR

Lucia Raatma received her bachelor's degree in English literature from the University of South Carolina and her master's degree in cinema studies from New York University. Both degrees taught her the power of stories, and very often she feels that the best stories are true ones. She found Charles Lindbergh's life to be full of excitement, intrigue, and more drama than any movie script could offer.

She has written a wide range of books for children and young adults. They include *Libraries* and *How Books Are Made* (Childrens Press); an eight-book general-safety series and a four-book fire-safety series (Bridgestone Books); and fourteen titles in a character-education series (Bridgestone Books). She has also written Career Biographies of Maya Angelou and Bill Gates for this series.

When she is not researching or writing, she enjoys going to movies, playing tennis, and spending time with her husband, daughter, and golden retriever.